Get in the tub

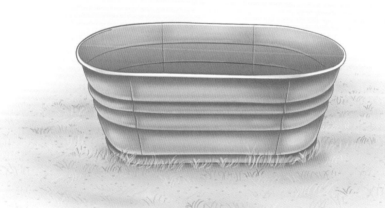

Pam is a mess.
She has mud on
her neck, back
and legs.

Sam gets the tub
and fills it.

Nat gets a bucket.

Sam rubs the
mud off Pam.

Nat gets rid of the suds.

Sid runs up to the tub. He taps Pam and runs off.

Pam is quick.
She tips the tub
and runs off.

Pam is back in the mud. Sam is too!

Sam is a mess. He has mud on his neck, back and legs.

Before reading

Say the sounds: c k ck j qu v w x y z zz ff ll ss

Practise blending the sounds: mess neck back fills bucket quick

High-frequency words: a on gets it in off up will get has his is of
Tricky words: she her and the to he no too
Vocabulary check: suds – froth or bubbles found in soapy water

Story discussion: Look at the cover. What is Sam doing? What do you think the tub is for?

Teaching points: Check that children can read the graphemes ck, qu, ff, ll, ss. Pick one or two of these graphemes and ask children to find and read a word with each in the book. Check that children can understand cause and effect (what happens and why). Check that they can identify and read the tricky words: she, her, and, the, to, he, no, too.

After reading

Comprehension:
- Who is the tub for?
- How do you think Nat feels when Pam runs off?
- Who is muddy at the end of the story?
- What might happen next?

Fluency: Speed-read the words again from the inside front cover.